This book belongs to:

_____

_____

For Alyn & Eleanor,
with love
Special thanks
to Jakob & Wilhelm
A.S.

For Jade & Eva
Happy adventuring!
B.D.

First published in 2011
by Meadowside Children's Books
185 Fleet Street, London EC4A 2HS
www.meadowsidebooks.com

Text © Amy Sparkes 2011
Illustrations © Benji Davies 2011

A CIP catalogue record for this book
is available from the British Library
1 2 3 4 5 6 7 8 9 10

Printed in China

Gruff's Guide to FAIRY TALE LAND

Written by **Billy G. Gruff**
& Amy Sparkes

Illustrated by **Benji Davies**

meadowside
CHILDREN'S BOOKS

Dear Reader,

Once upon a time, when I was a kid, I went looking for greener pastures with my brothers. One day we met a particularly nasty troll, but because of my amazing quick thinking (and head-butting skills), we escaped and didn't end up in the troll's huge hairy belly.

Not many people know their way around Fairy Tale Land so I have written this Gruff Guide to make your visit happier, your life span longer, and me richer! In this book, you will find all the information you need to survive Fairy Tale Land and with a bit of luck, you might even make it back for another visit!

Happy head-butting,

Mr Billy G. Gruff

P.s. Ever since crossing the bridge, I've fallen in love with exploring, and I have travelled to many weird and wonderful places. Look out for my other survival guides for young explorers!

CONTENTS

THIS WAY PLEASE!

GETTING THERE

Whatever you do, don't ask for directions to *Fairy Tale Land*, people will think you've gone mad. All you need is your favourite Fairy Tale and somewhere quiet to hide, preferably in a ring of toadstools but a wardrobe will do. Look at one of the pictures in your book. Really look, until you can smell the grass, hear the wind and feel the magic. Now, close your eyes, take a deep breath and make sure you're holding on to this guide book! Open your eyes, and your adventure begins...

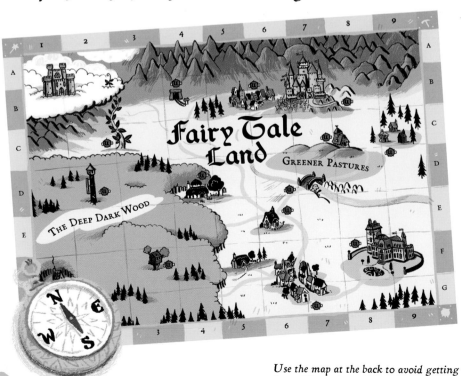

Use the map at the back to avoid getting lost while you're in Fairy Tale Land!

EXPLORER'S SURVIVAL KIT

If you're going to Fairy Tale Land, you'll need the following items.

1. Ice-pack
2. Extra thick gloves
3. Brightly coloured tights
   (preferably ladder-proof)
4. Fire extinguisher
5. Clothes peg
6. Parachute
7. Bag of marshmallows
8. Sugar cubes
9. Hairpin
10. Bright-coloured bead necklace
11. Scissors
12. Book of Baby names

WHERE NOT TO STAY

Safe places to stay are rare, so book early. Cinderella's Palace Hotel has beautiful ballrooms and all beds are P.E.A. (see p46 for more information). Three Little Pigs holiday cottages are comfortable - Brick Cottage is safest. Snow White's Tea Rooms take guests, but the beds are rather small. (See map at back for all.) Even if these are booked, DO NOT stay at the following places:

GINGERBREAD GUEST HOUSE

The owner, Mrs I.B.A. Widge enjoys feeding her guests, but what she doesn't tell you is that you're next on the menu! The 'bedroom' locks on the outside, although it doesn't actually have a bed, and isn't so much a room as a cage. Also, the constant roaring fire in the oven makes the Guest House horribly hot.

VACANCIES

SURVIVAL TIPS

★ MAKE SURE YOU HAVE THE HAIRPIN IN YOUR SURVIVAL KIT TO HAND.

★ USE THE HAIRPIN WHEN THE WITCH ASKS TO FEEL YOUR FINGER TO SEE IF YOU STILL NEED FATTENING UP OR IF YOU'RE READY TO BE EATEN. HANSEL USED A BONE, BUT A HAIRPIN WILL GET YOU MORE PUDDING!

★ BE SURE TO KEEP YOUR SURVIVAL KIT FIRE EXTINGUISHER HANDY IN CASE YOU END UP BEING SHOVED TOWARDS A HOT OVEN. (THE FOAM ONES ARE BEST. AIM IT AT THE FIRE, THEN ENJOY AIMING IT AT THE WITCH!)

Remember not to stay here alone
- you'll need someone to rescue you.
A sister makes an ideal travelling companion.

TOWER HOTEL

As soon as you arrive, you will find yourself trapped on the top floor. The room has a view, but no door. For a real Fairy Tale Land experience, get Rapunzel's Hair Extensions first (see Ugly Sisters Beauty Salon, p23) and then arrange the services of a Prince (p30).

SURVIVAL TIPS

- BE WARNED EXTRA LONG HAIR WILL ALLOW PRINCES UP, BUT IT WON'T HELP YOU DOWN.

- YOU CAN GET A GOOD NIGHT'S SLEEP HERE BUT BE SURE TO PULL YOUR HAIR UP FIRST - ANYONE CAN CLIMB IN, NOT JUST PRINCES.

- KEEP YOUR SURVIVAL KIT SCISSORS HANDY IN CASE OF AN UNWELCOME VISITOR.

- WHEN YOU'VE HAD A GOOD NIGHT'S SLEEP, USE THE SURVIVAL KIT PARACHUTE TO ESCAPE AND DON'T RETURN. YOU MIGHT NOT BE SO LUCKY NEXT TIME!

Let your hair down at Tower Hotel (but be careful who you let up!)

THREE BEARS B&B

Mr and Mrs Bear can be a bit grizzly, and if you put one foot out of line, you may end up being chased into the woods and never seen again.

The breakfast menu here is limited. Don't ask for cornflakes, and whatever you do, be polite about the porridge.

The Three Bears B&B Special

Your choice of Bed

Your choice of Chair

& Porridge how YOU like it

Only one of the beds here is P.E.A.
(see p46 for more information).

(see p46 for more information).

SURVIVAL TIP

SNEAK SOME HONEY INTO THE BEARS' PORRIDGE AT BREAKFAST. IT MIGHT JUST SWEETEN THEM UP A LITTLE.

It's best not to be in bed when the bears come home...

R.E.A Approved

B&B

13

WAYS NOT TO GET AROUND

You may like the idea of travelling using Fairy Tale Land transport, but using your own two legs is usually the safest and most reliable way of moving. Here are some things to avoid:

THE SEVEN DWARVES TUNNEL NETWORK

There is an Underground in Fairy Tale Land, but it was dug by dwarves when diamonds were rare and they needed extra cash. The enchanted mine-carts may seem a fun way to travel, but they have a mind of their own and you never know where you'll end up!

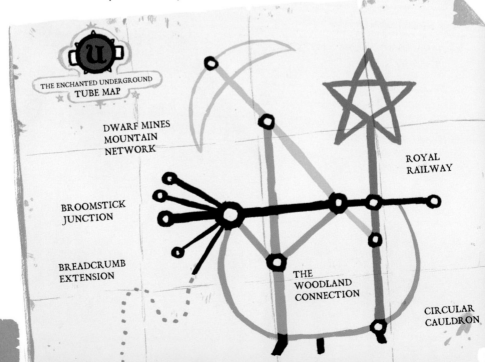

THE ENCHANTED UNDERGROUND
TUBE MAP

DWARF MINES
MOUNTAIN
NETWORK

ROYAL
RAILWAY

BROOMSTICK
JUNCTION

BREADCRUMB
EXTENSION

THE
WOODLAND
CONNECTION

CIRCULAR
CAULDRON

PUMPKIN COACHES

If you're out late, you could find
yourself stranded with nothing
but a large vegetable. Still,
at least you won't starve.

PRINCE'S FAITHFUL STEED

So ridiculously expensive,
that you get taken for a
ride in more ways than one.
And the Prince keeps his dazzling,
white stallion and gives you a
grumpy old donkey anyway.

BROOMSTICK TAXIS

These taxis look like fun,
but they tend to fly straight
to the nearest witch's lair —
never to return.

CREATURES NOT TO MEET

There are many nice creatures in Fairy Tale Land, such as fairy godmothers, friendly woodcutters and extremely handsome goats, but there are many dangerous beasties too. Avoid the following creatures and check out the survival tips for advice on how to deal with baddies before they deal with you:

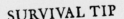

TROLL *(Trollius uglius)*

WATCH OUT:
In caves; under rickety-rackety bridges.

WHAT THEY EAT:
Anything — particularly fond of goat.

WHAT THEY FEAR:
Clever goats and water. They never wash, and can't swim. (It's a bit stupid of them to live under bridges, but that's trolls for you.)

SURVIVAL TIP

TROLLS ARE STUPID AND EASILY TRICKED. IF YOU MEET ONE, SAY, "MY BROTHER'S COMING NEXT, AND HE'S FATTER THAN ME," (EVEN IF HE ISN'T). TROLLS' EARS ARE FILLED WITH EARWAX SO SHOUT OR IT WILL JUST EAT YOU ANYWAY. IF THIS FAILS, LOWER YOUR HEAD, CHARGE AND HEAD-BUTT IT INTO THE RIVER. (HAVE YOUR ICE-PACK READY AS YOU MIGHT GET A HEADACHE). TRAIN WITH WORLD HEAD-BUTTING CHAMPION BILLY GRUFF JUNIOR FOR BEST RESULTS (SEE P35).

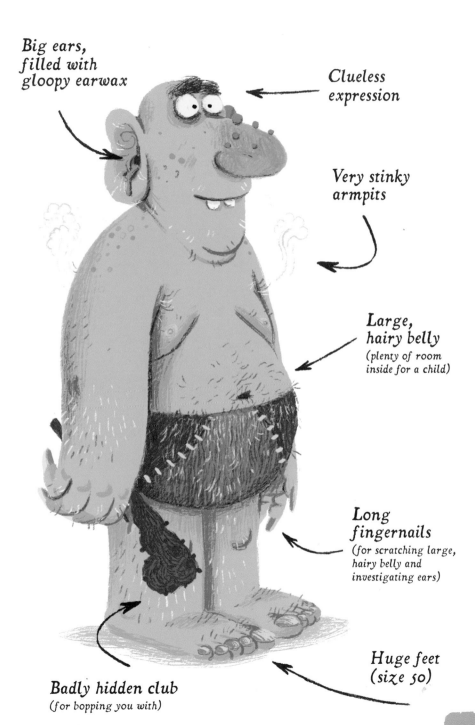

Big ears,
filled with
gloopy earwax

Clueless
expression

Very stinky
armpits

Large,
hairy belly
(plenty of room
inside for a child)

Long
fingernails
(for scratching large,
hairy belly and
investigating ears)

Huge feet
(size 50)

Badly hidden club
(for bopping you with)

Long snout
*(all the better for
smelling you with)*

Sharp yellow teeth
(never been brushed)

Beady eyes

Bad breath
*(this will actually knock you
out before the sharp yellow
teeth come near you)*

**Ticklish
armpits**
(very important)

Wilting flowers
*(a sign a wolf has
passed by)*

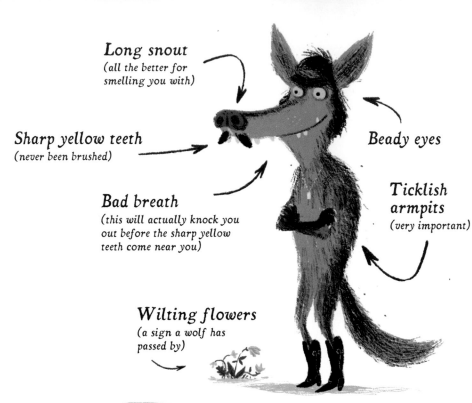

WOLF *(Wolfius lickchopius)*

WATCH OUT:
In woods;
near pig villages.

WHAT THEY EAT:
Little girls;
grandmothers; pigs.

WHAT THEY FEAR:
Kickboxing grannies;
looking stupid,
especially in front of pigs.

SURVIVAL TIPS

 YOU WILL SMELL THE WOLF'S TERRIBLE BREATH A MILE OFF. PUT THE SURVIVAL KIT CLOTHES PEG ON YOUR NOSE TO ESCAPE THE DREADED 'BAD BREATH DEATH' (SEE P46).

 IF A WOLF POUNCES, GO FOR THE ARMPITS AS THEY ARE VERY TICKLISH. FEELING EMBARRASSED, IT WILL RUN OFF TO HIDE IN THE WOOD. BUT BE WARNED, IT MIGHT COME BACK TO LOOK FOR SUPPER, POSSIBLY DRESSED AS YOUR GRANNY. BOOK A PLACE ON GRANDMA HOOD'S SELF-DEFENCE COURSE, (P36) TO BE ON THE SAFE SIDE.

Black, pointy hat

Greasy hair

Dreadful
make-up
*(from Ugly Sisters
Beauty Salon, p23)*

Silly shoes
*(supposed to be
scary-looking)*

Crooked
nose
*(usually caused
by falling off
broomstick)*

Large
'beauty'
warts

WITCH (Haggius wartius)

WATCH OUT:
In dark, shadowy
places; woods.

WHAT THEY EAT:
You; sugar cubes.

WHAT THEY FEAR:
Being shut in hot ovens;
not looking their worst;
people not noticing their
horrible shoes.

SURVIVAL TIPS

 THE WITCH IS A CUNNING ENEMY, BUT ALL WITCHES HAVE A WEAK SPOT, THEY ARE VERY SENSITIVE ABOUT THEIR LOOKS. THEY SPEND HOURS GREASING THEIR LANK HAIR, WORRYING ABOUT WHETHER THEY HAVE TOO MANY TEETH AND MAKING SURE THEY LOOK AWFUL AND SCARY.

IF YOU ARE UNLUCKY ENOUGH TO MEET ONE ON YOUR TRAVELS, TELL HER YOU THINK HER TEETH LOOK NICE. AS SHE DISSOLVES INTO PANIC, OFFER HER SOME SUGAR TO ROT THEM A BIT MORE AND THEN RUN FOR YOUR LIFE.

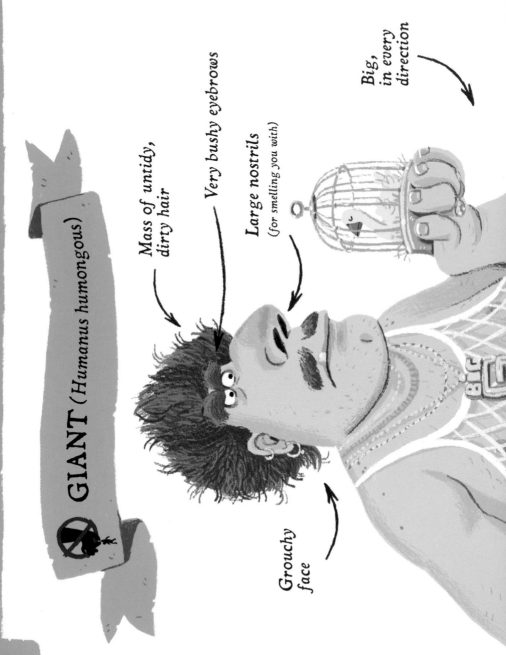

GIANT (*Humanus humongous*)

Mass of untidy, dirty hair

Very bushy eyebrows

Large nostrils
(*for smelling you with*)

Grouchy face

Big, in every direction

SURVIVAL TIP

IF YOU DARE TO GO BEANSTALK-CLIMBING, YOU NEED TO BE FIT. GIANTS ARE STUPID, BUT DANGEROUS! TRAIN WITH GINGER BREADMAN FOR FITNESS (SEE P14), AND ENROL ON JACK'S BEANSTALK EXPERIENCE (P37). IF YOU MEET THE GIANT, TELL HIM YOUR NAME IS JACK OR JACKIE AND HE MIGHT NOT CHASE YOU. IF HE DOES CHASE YOU, USE YOUR SURVIVAL KIT PARACHUTE TO GET TO THE BOTTOM BEFORE HIM! IT IS ADVISABLE TO TAKE A WOODCUTTER WITH YOU TO CHOP THE BEANSTALK DOWN AFTERWARDS (SEE P3).

WATCH OUT:

In castles; up beanstalks.

WHAT THEY EAT:

Little children; golden eggs; roast magic chicken.

WHAT THEY FEAR:

Axes; boys called Jack; falling from a great height.

Lots of gold jewellery

WHERE NOT TO SHOP

There are plenty of fun and interesting things to buy in Fairy Tale Land, but there are also many seemingly innocent shops that could land you in the lap of trouble. If you go to *Pumpkin Parade*, be careful of the following shops:

PRINCELY FASHIONS

Only go here if you have really bad dress sense, are planning a fancy dress party or you need to buy a gift for an uncle you don't like. The last thing you want to do is look like a prince (see p30).

THE
UGLY SISTERS
BEAUTY SALON

Remember, beauty is in the eye of the beholder, and these two are the beholders...

The Ugly Sisters 'Beauty Salon' should really be called an 'Ugly Salon'. The only hair product of any use is Rapunzel's Hair Extensions, useful if you have booked into Tower Hotel (p12).

SURVIVAL TIPS

 AVOID THEIR SPECIAL OFFERS FOR HAIRDRESSING – YOU WILL LOOK LIKE A GIANT WITH A BAD PERM WHO GOT STRUCK BY LIGHTNING

 DO NOT LET THEM USE THE 'SLIME 'N' GRIME' HAIR GEL UNLESS YOU WANT TO LOOK LIKE A GREASY WITCH WHO'S BEEN DRAGGED UP A BEANSTALK BACKWARDS.

 DO NOT GET THE 'SPECIAL MAKEOVER' – YOU WILL LOOK FAR MORE HIDEOUS THAT WHEN YOU WENT IN (SEE WITCH, P19).

JUMBO FACE CREAM

Shampoo
WASHING UP LIQUID

SLIME 'N' GRIME

Miss Widge's Home Made Sweets

The Witch isn't the only unsavoury thing here!

This stall brings a new meaning to the word homemade. These are not made AT home, but rather FROM her home (see p10–11). These are to be avoided for one important reason. Mrs Widge does not like children (except with roast potatoes and peas) so her sweets are made to tease, not please.

SURVIVAL TIPS

* PEPPERMINTS. THEY LOOK HARMLESS, BUT THEY ARE REALLY CHILLI-PEPPER MINTS. THEY'RE SO HOT YOU'LL NEED YOUR FIRE EXTINGUISHER FOR YOUR TONGUE.

* LOLLISPOTS. THESE WILL HAVE YOU BREAKING OUT IN PIMPLES BEFORE YOU CAN RUN TO THE UGLY SISTERS BEAUTY SALON FOR EMERGENCY MAKE-UP!

* DOUGHNUT SURPRISE. DELICIOUS ON THE OUTSIDE, BUT INSTEAD OF NICE GOOEY JAM INSIDE, EXPECT A NICE GOOEY SLUG.

The Poisoned

APPLE

*What's in a name?
In this case, everything
you need to know.*

To say the food here is 'a bit dodgy' is like saying Snow White's stepmother was 'a bit naughty'. Do not be tempted by the smell of apple pie wafting in the breeze. Eat here and it will be your last supper.

WHERE NOT TO EXPLORE

Never go exploring in Fairy Tale Land by yourself, you never know who or what you might find and you'll usually end up under an evil spell. If you do go exploring, these are the places not to visit:

SLEEPING BEAUTY'S CASTLE

Many visitors are drawn to this beautiful building, but only go if you are on good terms with a Fairy Godmother, (p33). The last thing you want is to bump into the Wicked Fairy who needs help with a spot of spinning!
Keep your marshmallows handy.

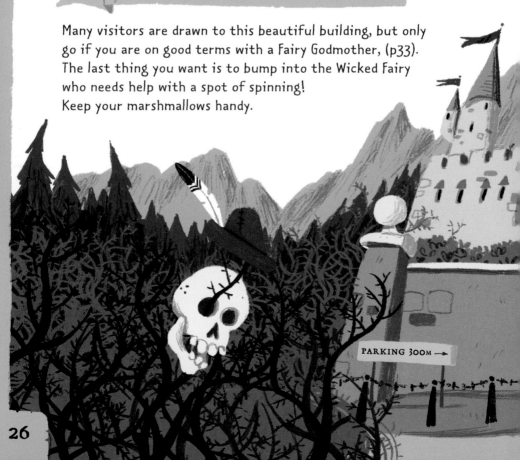

PARKING 300M →

SURVIVAL TIPS

 WEAR THE EXTRA THICK GLOVES FROM YOUR SURVIVAL KIT IN CASE YOU FALL UNDER A SPELL AND HAVE A DESPERATE URGE TO TOUCH A SPINNING WHEEL.

 BUY A HIGH QUALITY PILLOW AT THE GODMOTHERS' GIFT SHOP AT THE CASTLE ENTRANCE, JUST IN CASE. IF YOU'RE GOING TO FALL ASLEEP FOR ONE HUNDRED YEARS, YOU NEED A DECENT PILLOW OR YOU'LL WAKE UP WITH A VERY STIFF NECK.

 THE GIFT SHOP ALSO SELLS ANTI-WRINKLE CREAM TO HELP REDUCE THE SHOCK WHEN YOU WAKE UP ONE HUNDRED YEARS OLDER.

 IF YOU'RE THINKING OF VISITING THE CASTLE TO RESCUE A PRINCESS AND YOU WANT TO DO IT FAIRY TALE LAND STYLE, YOU'LL NEED A HORSE (PRINCE'S FAITHFUL STEEDS, P15) AND AN AXE TO CHOP THROUGH THE BRAMBLES (ASK EDWARD CUTTER IF YOU CAN BORROW HIS, P31).

Weary travellers beware of napping here!

CASTLE & GIFT SHOP **OPEN**

THE DEEP DARK WOOD

Little Red Riding Hood, Hansel and Gretel, Snow White, Goldilocks… all of them wandered off into the woods alone. Don't do it. You'll definitely get lost, you'll probably be followed by some horrible creature (see p16–21) and you might get gobbled up by a wolf (p18). If you really must explore the woods, use Edward Cutter's Woodland Tours, (see p31) to avoid ending up as Sunday Roast.

SURVIVAL TIPS

- YOU'LL BE SAFE IF YOU FOLLOW THE SOUND OF HAPPY SINGING, AS BADDIES CAN NEVER SING IN TUNE.

- IN ORDER TO REALLY INCREASE YOUR CHANCES OF SURVIVAL IN THE DEEP DARK WOOD, TAKE GRANDMA HOOD'S SELF-DEFENCE CLASS (SEE P36).

BREADCRUMB TRAIL

The Breadcrumb Trail may start off signposted but it is not safe (see p47 for more information). Signs soon disappear and you will go round and round in circles and probably end up feeling very sad and alone. However, worse than this, you'll probably end up at Gingerbread Guest House (p10–11), which is bad news. The Pebble Trail is slightly safer, but it's still not reliable and once it's dark, it too will lead you to Gingerbread Guesthouse.

BURP!

SURVIVAL TIP

IF YOU ARE LOST, BREAK THE NECKLACE FROM YOUR SURVIVAL KIT AND LEAVE A TRAIL OF BRIGHT BEADS BEHIND YOU. THEY'LL BE EASIER TO SEE THAN STONES AND LESS LIKELY TO BE EATEN BY BIRDS THAN BREAD.

WHO'S WHO
OF FAIRY TALE LAND

Knowing who's who in Fairy Tale Land can make all the difference for a safe trip. Here are the most important people to know:

Whiffy
(too much aftershave)

Smug smirk and gold-capped teeth →

Well, hello!

Scrawny build
(he always get others to do his work)

KEY INFORMATION
Prince Charming is THE person to know in Fairy Tale Land. He can kiss you awake from a magical sleep; rescue you from towers and even make you feel good about your own clothes. To call him, wave the dazzling tights from your Survival Kit around. They'll catch his eye and he's always laddering his, so he'll be extra grateful that they're ladder-proof!

Tights and knee-high boots
(considered acceptable) ←

PRINCE CHARMING

Contact Mr Edward Cutter to arrange a safe tour of the woods (see p28-29)

Edward Cutter
Woodland Tours & Forestry

BEANSTALK CHOPPER OF THE YEAR

"NO WOOD TOO DEEP AND DARK"

tel: 0800-INTO-THE-WOODS
(Ask for Woody)

Scruffy, dirty clothes

Whiffy
(spends money on axes not soap)

Kind smile
(loves all creatures, great and small)

Big bulging muscles
(from chopping wood all day)

Axe in hand
(won't even part with it at night. Mrs Cutter is not pleased)

KEY INFORMATION

If you see Edward Cutter, try not to hold your nose. He is kind, helpful and unlikely to push you into a hot oven, but he doesn't have the best personal hygiene. Edward Cutter can chop down beanstalks, lead you safely out of the wood and wolves aren't that keen on him either. To find him, follow signs saying 'firewood for sale' or just follow your nose!

EDWARD CUTTER

Scary eyebrows
(Ugly Sisters Beauty Salon, p23)

Wings with sharp, spiky bits

Long pointy nose
(sticks in other people's business)

Smoking wand
(not a good sign)

Dark clothes
(make her look more evil)

KEY INFORMATION

Renowned for casting mean spells on happy people and spoiling perfectly pleasant christenings, the Wicked Fairy has a nasty temper and if you don't know how to handle her, you'll be under an evil spell yourself before you can say, 'bibbety-bobbety-boo'. She is usually looking to spoil someone's happiness, so if you see her, be sure to look as glum as possible and she should leave you alone.

WICKED FAIRY

Soft pink clothes
(by The Marshmallow Company)

Signs of forgetfulness
(misplaced wand; lost marshmallow
tucked behind ear)

Friendly face

Sparkly wand
(a good sign)

KEY INFORMATION

She is kind and helpful and can solve almost any problem, but because of this, she is very busy and finding her isn't always easy. If you need her, leave your Survival Kit marshmallows somewhere quiet and she should magically appear. She loves marshmallows — soft, sweet and pink, just like her. While she nibbles away ask her to be your Fairy Godmother, it's hard to say, 'I'm a bit busy, dear' with a mouthful of marshmallow.

FAIRY GODMOTHER

On your entry to Fairy Tale Land, it is a very good idea to enrol in some courses to boost your chances of staying alive:

GINGER

NEEDS YOU!

Enrol **NOW** and do 300 press-ups while you're at it !!

Your enemies may run, run, run as fast as they can, but they'll never catch you, if you train with Ginger Breadman.

GRUFF BROS.

SCHOOL OF
HEAD-BUTTING

≈ World Famous ≈
TROLL FLIPPING TECHNIQUE
explained and demonstrated by our expert

BILLY JUNIOR

Run by my brother, Billy Junior. Send trolls flying into the middle of next week (watch out if you're staying for a fortnight). For safety reasons, head-butting is practiced on rocks instead of real trolls. Helmets and First Aid included.

Learn from the expert and never worry about wolves again (see p18). Special Wolf-Wrestling Demonstrations are also run when she's caught one stupid enough to sneak into her bed (make sure you have your survival kit clothes peg to hand).

GRANDMA HOOD'S SELF-DEFENCE CLASS

- KICKBOXING TIPS
- TICKLING MASTERCLASS
- WOLF-WRESTLING
- TEA & CAKE

FEATHER DUSTERS WILL BE PROVIDED

Jack's Beanstalk Experience

Climb your way to a Great Day Out!

Learn how to climb safely, chop quickly and parachute smoothly for a safe trip up – and down – a beanstalk. The parachute lessons are useful if you end up trapped at Tower Hotel (see p12).

WHAT NOT TO EAT

Not all food and drink in Fairy Tale Land is safe. Some can have dreadful effects on you, and others are best avoided unless you want to be in trouble with the residents. Here's what not to eat or drink:

1. **Snow White's Special Juice**
(not foul or dangerous but so sickly sweet you'll feel quite awful!)

2. **Sweets or biscuits**
(could be from Gingerbread Guest House and enchanted, dangerous or tasting of smoked witch. Yuck!)

3. **Apples**
(go for a pear instead, no-one ever poisons pears)

4. Gingerbread men
(could be a relative of Miss Ginger Breadman
who is black belt in karate)

5. Beans on Toast
(could be magic beans)

6. Pumpkins
(could be someone's coach)

7. Green Juice
(do you really want
to drink something
from a cauldron
that looks like
liquidised frog?)

8. Porridge
(usually too hot, or too
cold, rarely just right)

EVENTS TO MISS

There are many safe events which run throughout the Fairy Tale Land year: Pumpkin-Coach Racing and Ugly Sisters Magical Makeover, to name a few (see p46 - 47 for more information on both). However, the following are ones best missed:

PRINCE'S FASHION SHOW

ALL PROCEEDS
TO NEW CLOTHES
FOR PRINCES

Being forced to watch so many displays of hideous clothes will probably put you off your supper. Only attend if you are in desperate need of a prince's help and have super-strength sunglasses to dull the brightness of the clothes.

SPINNING WORKSHOP

It's a must-have this season!

Spinning wheels in Fairy Tale Land are dangerous and the workshop is almost always run by the Wicked Fairy (see p32). Try sewing instead. Cinderella is an expert housekeeper, and runs courses on dressmaking and sewing. If she can teach mice and bluebirds to do it, she can teach you.

POTION TASTING FESTIVAL

VOLUNTEERS WANTED

Avoid this unless you fancy being changed into a purple dragon. Good for scaring your little sister, but not good for much else.

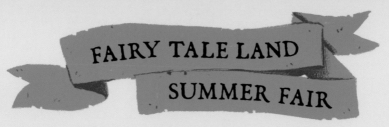

FAIRY TALE LAND
SUMMER FAIR

This is a real treat and all the residents turn out for it.
Although most of the events are quite safe,
be warned about the following:

COCONUT SHY

These are actually the giant's
golden eggs. If he catches you
he'll drag you up the beanstalk
for lunch before you can say,
"Fi, fie, fo, fum."

PUSS IN BOOTS'
WELLY-WANGING STALL

This sounds harmless but can be
a dangerous affair for cats.
(The prize is coveted though, see p47)

Hall of
Mirrors

Dragon
Rides

GUESS
MY
NAME

GUESS THE NAME OF THE MAN

Ever since the Queen guessed right and he lost his game, Rumpelstiltskin has been looking for a new name. Give him your Book of Baby Names and leave!

APPLE BOBBING

Don't take part unless you want a bowl of water and a red apple to be the last thing you ever see.

THE HALL OF MIRRORS

These mirrors are enchanted, deadly and worst of all, make your nose look big.

WHAT NOT TO SAY

As with everywhere you go in Fairy Tale Land, there are certain things you really shouldn't say to certain people. Knowing this could save your life, so take note and avoid saying the following things:

"Have you tried mouthwash?"

"I had some beautiful scrambled golden eggs this morning."

"I like your shoes. Did you steal them from the circus?"

"Did you know there's a spot, right there, on the side of your nose?"

"Actually, your shirt... it clashes with your tights."

GLOSSARY

BAD BREATH DEATH

A particularly nasty way to go, as you slowly rot from the nose down. People think it was the STRENGTH of the wolf's breath which huffed and puffed the Three Little Pigs' Houses down, but no, it was the foul STENCH of it which simply rotted the building material in seconds.

P.E.A. STAMP OF QUALITY

Princess Ella is particularly fussy about her beds and is famous for having felt a pea through several mattresses. She set up her own mattress company so that no other poor, spoilt princess would have a bad nights' sleep ever again. (Plus she's made enough money to fulfil her dream: a lifetime supply of white chocolate mice).

PUMPKIN-COACH RACING

A double-race. Firstly, a race among coaches to see who is first across the finish line. Secondly, a race against the clock because it starts at 11.57pm. If you decide to enter, wear full waterproofs and be prepared to spend the night inside a pumpkin. If you're not finished by midnight, you won't be racing your coach, you'll be living in it.

FROG KISSING

This is popular with visitors, although most of the residents of Fairy Tale Land know better. There are very few genuine Frog Princes left, so the chances are, you'll kiss bumpy, green, slimy lips for nothing. Trust me, there are better things to do with your time. Picking your nose, for example.

WELLY-WANGING

Whoever throws their welly the furthest wins the Puss-in-Boots Golden Welly Trophy. Watch out for vengeful cats afterwards though.

UGLY SISTERS MAGICAL MAKEOVER

Excellent entertainment. The magical element is that they manage to make everyone look like a witch or an evil fairy, even if you looked perfectly normal beforehand. Learn useful tips — perfect for giving your mum a fright!

PEBBLE TRAIL

Donated by Hansel and Gretel after they escaped Mrs Widge and set up their own consultancy business.

BREADCRUMB TRAIL

The old, original trail — well, what's left of it — from Hansel and Gretel's first trip into the woods. Most of it was eaten by birds almost as soon as Hansel dropped the crumbs. Hard to follow, so lots of people get lost on it, and it is therefore a hot spot for wolves.

Fairy Tale Land
MAP KEY

FOOTPATHS

HILLS

WATERWAYS

MOUNTAINS

FOREST AND WOODLAND

UNDERGROUND STOPS

Dwarf Mine Entrance	B4
Ed Cutter's Woodland Tours HQ	F3
Giant's Golden Castle	A1
Gingerbread Guest House	F1
Grandma Hood's House	F5
Gruff Bros Ltd.	C8
Jack's Beanstalk Experience	C3
Palace Hotel & Gingerbread Gym	F8
Pumpkin Parade Shops	F6
Sleeping Beauty's Castle	B7
Snow White's Tea Rooms	D4
The Poisoned Apple	F6
Three Bears B&B	E6
Tower Hotel	D2
Troll-Bridge Crossing	D7
Three Pigs Holiday Cottages	C9

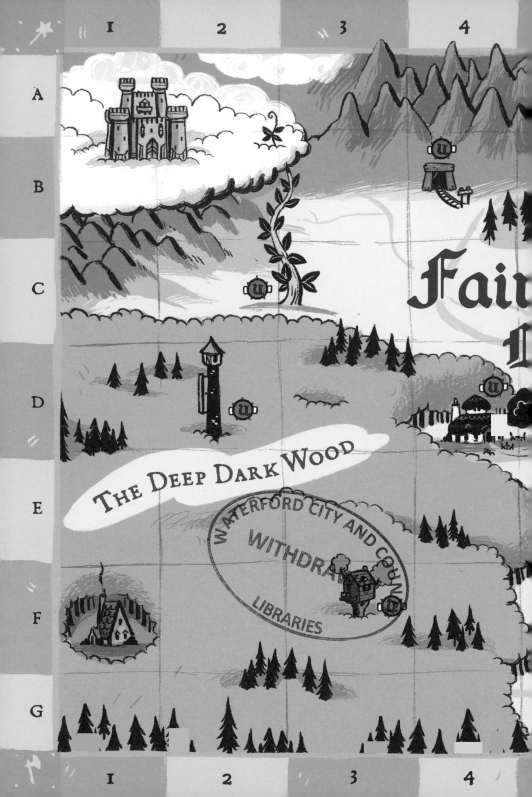